The Book of JANE

Winner of the Iowa Poetry Prize

The Book of JANE

Jennifer Habel

University of Iowa Press <> Iowa City

University of Iowa Press, Iowa City 52242
Copyright © 2020 by Jennifer Habel
www.uipress.uiowa.edu
Printed in the United States of America
Design by Sara T. Sauers
Printed on acid-free paper

Cover image is from "Thursday Nights Out" by Leanne Shapton, originally
published in the *New York Times*. Copyright © 2011 by Leanne Shapton, used
by permission of The Wylie Agency LLC.

Library of Congress Cataloging-in-Publication Data
Names: Habel, Jennifer, author.
Title: The book of Jane / Jennifer Habel.
Description: Iowa City: University of Iowa Press, [2020] |
Series: Iowa poetry prize | "Winner of the Iowa Poetry Prize."
Identifiers: LCCN 2019037877 (print) | LCCN 2019037878 (ebook) |
ISBN 9781609387075 (paperback) | ISBN 9781609387082 (ebook)
Subjects: LCGFT: Poetry.
Classification: LCC PS3608.A2375 B66 2020 (print) |
LCC PS3608.A2375 (ebook) | DDC 811/.6—dc23
LC record available at https://lccn.loc.gov/2019037877
LC ebook record available at https://lccn.loc.gov/2019037878

Dick said, "I see it.
I see the big ball."

Jane said, "Oh, Dick.
I want the little ball.
Find the little ball."

—*We Come and Go*

CONTENTS

Jane and the Relative Adverb 1

<>

Einstein's Dinner 5
Jane and the Bushel 7
Jane's Desk 8
Seven Students 10
The Art Room 12
Examples of the Interrogative in Jane's Kitchen 13
Jane's Shame 14
Jane in the Guest Room 15
The Pedestal 16
Carte Blanche 17
A Guide to Jane's Office 18

<>

Jane in the Passenger Seat 23
Diagnosis: Jane 24
Jane Alone 25
The Obstetrician's Lesson 26
The Doll in the Convent 27
Warp and Weft 28
Questions on Jane's Birthday 30
Mary's Year 31

<>

Jane in the Interlude 51
Jane and the Escapes 52
A Concept of Service 53
Examples of the Declarative in Jane's Kitchen 54
Life-Sized Portrait 55
Examples of the Imperative in Jane's Kitchen 56
The Ballet Master 57
The Vocation of Saint Thérèse 58
Basic Reader 59
A Small Movement of Freedom inside of Fate 60
Jane and the Visitors 62
Jane's Souvenir 63

<>

Matisse's Great-Granddaughter, or Jane and the Long Way 67

The Book of JANE

JANE AND THE RELATIVE ADVERB

Inside "where"
is "here"

and inside "here"
is "her"

and inside "her"
is
       —"Wait, *what* is 'where'?"
Jane hears.

"An adverb,"
Jane avers.

("Where" is "her"
inside "we,"

she sees.)

EINSTEIN'S DINNER

A single bite from the center of each of six lamb chops
was Einstein's dinner.

He did not like fat.
Or waste.

He gave the remainders to his sister, his daughter,
his lover. . . .

His lover's husband was, like Einstein, a gentle man.
A sculptor, Russian, he worked

on West 8th, though, like Einstein, lived
in the immensity of the cosmos.

He made swan-shaped chairs, dwarves
taking tea, wooden boxes with wooden keys,

saints and girls and nudes. *A child full of wonder*,
recalled his model. *A saint*

seeing the macrocosm in every tiny piece of life. While she posed
a mouse stood on her shoe.

For Einstein's lover's husband fed them.
He fed the cockroaches, too. He set bowls of sugar

on tables in the shapes of woodland creatures.
Thirty-odd mice, innumerable cockroaches

in a West Village studio. Fortunately for the neighbors
Einstein's lover's husband had a wife.

In Russian, she sent her husband to the park;
in English, she spoke to the exterminators.

She spoke five languages, or seven.
At any rate, a lot.

Einstein wrote to her in German:
Ich wusch mir alleine den Kopf—I washed my head

by myself. But not, he wrote, with the greatest success;
I am not as careful as you are.

Indeed: she brought a boiled chicken to Penn Station.
Einstein's train arrived at noon. He might be hungry

and he did not like sandwiches
or restaurants. She was most careful

that he not be bothered—in the garden, for example.
Geniuses like gardens. There they can

solve problems or feed the birds.

JANE AND THE BUSHEL

Jane is smart, but not as smart as her husband.

Jane was smart, but not as smart as her father.

Jane is smart enough to know her mother

should not have let Jane know

that Jane's derelict brother outscored Jane

on the IQ test. Sometimes you have to hide

your light under a bushel, Jane once heard

a professor tell his junior colleague.

His colleague couldn't stop talking. She couldn't

stop talking because she wasn't pretty.

When a pretty woman gets old

she sometimes starts talking. Jane might

be getting ready when she hides

before the mirror plucking

her new gray hairs.

JANE'S DESK

Before it was white
it was black.

Before it was black
it was blue.

Before it was blue
it was

unfinished—
would

that it were
practical,

this small, pretty,
impractical

desk: on which
Jane placed

a dish; in which
she stored

a sewing kit;
over which

she hung
a wrinkled print;

at which she
did not write

her master's thesis.
(That was written

at the kitchen table.)
A desk for ornament

and etiquette.
For the expression

of sympathy
and gratitude

and glad tidings.
In short,

a desk for others.
Now it is Jane's

daughter's desk.
At which

her daughter
does not sit.

There is not
even a chair.

Jane stares—
beneath the paint

the knots rise.

SEVEN STUDENTS

When I was a child I thought the answers to tests had to be transmitted to a person through some kind of food

Another memory is of the kindergarten teacher saying "Good-bye, children," at the end of the day, and my envy of the girl whose name I assumed to be Children

In any case, it seems I was always preparing myself for tests, or thought I was

Who was I, anyway? What was I supposed to do?

If anything, I just thought I was not an unusual person, and in retrospect, I wasn't

I thought everything that needed to be written had already been written or would be

but to try to get at things from an angle—nothing very grand, just a little twist

Showing off to straight men remained a delight and necessity to women of my generation

That little twist always got me an A minus

When I was going off to college, I got two copies of this thing, this impossibly neurotic, very strange book by this woman who'd been working on it her whole life

I guess my parents read a review somewhere and thought, You know, well, Joy thinks she's going to be a writer

It's the same sort of thing that makes rats fall over on their sides in Skinner boxes

My mother sent me an ad she'd clipped out of a newspaper, and she said, Anybody can get into this school, and I think you better go to it

It was my secret hope that someday the teacher would say, "Good-bye, Janet"

I was the most ordinary of the ordinary

I was obsessed with Dickinson

I was uneasy with my presence in life

The habit of attention getting stays with you

So I just lay still on the porch all day and read Eugene O'Neill

More about women and men?

If the rat finds there's nothing it can do effectively, the rat will give up

Maybe we should move on to a new subject

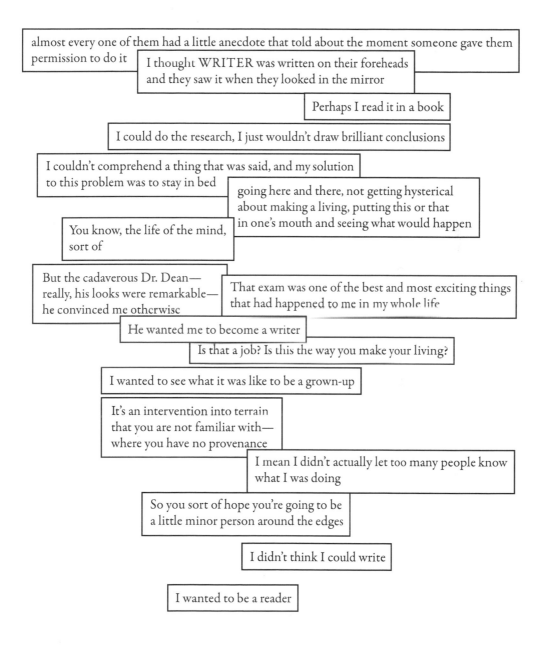

almost every one of them had a little anecdote that told about the moment someone gave them permission to do it

I thought WRITER was written on their foreheads and they saw it when they looked in the mirror

Perhaps I read it in a book

I could do the research, I just wouldn't draw brilliant conclusions

I couldn't comprehend a thing that was said, and my solution to this problem was to stay in bed

going here and there, not getting hysterical about making a living, putting this or that in one's mouth and seeing what would happen

You know, the life of the mind, sort of

But the cadaverous Dr. Dean— really, his looks were remarkable— he convinced me otherwise

That exam was one of the best and most exciting things that had happened to me in my whole life

He wanted me to become a writer

Is that a job? Is this the way you make your living?

I wanted to see what it was like to be a grown-up

It's an intervention into terrain that you are not familiar with— where you have no provenance

I mean I didn't actually let too many people know what I was doing

So you sort of hope you're going to be a little minor person around the edges

I didn't think I could write

I wanted to be a reader

From interviews with
E. Hardwick / T. Morrison / J. Malcolm / J. Didion / J. Williams / A. Beattie / D. Eisenberg

THE ART ROOM

Wearing matching jumpers,
making paper flowers—

Good, they hear. *Pretty*.

And aren't their mothers pretty?
And aren't their mothers good?

The mothers will love
their indistinguishable gifts.

Just ask them.

EXAMPLES OF THE INTERROGATIVE
IN JANE'S KITCHEN

Is the fifth sense talking?

How do you do a capital G?

I have to, don't I?

Do you want to be just like me?

Why did you put on makeup to go to the grocery store?

Why don't you wear your boots?

Is this really better than taking the pills?

Can we just start with what we have?

JANE'S SHAME

If a child needs a band-aid and his mother doesn't have one
Jane has one. It is deep

in the zippered compartment of her purse, its wrapper
worn as an old dollar.

Matches, bottle opener, tweezers, ibuprofen.
Nail file, bug spray, chapstick, sunblock.

Jane never did buy the tool to break
her sinking car's window.

Whatever happened to her Swiss Army knife
with all its clever integrity?

Simone's dad is early
for Ballet pickup. Is this, he asks, a refugee camp

for mothers?

JANE IN THE GUEST ROOM

Jane wants to wear the necklace she brought: it would please
her mother. But everything that pleases

Jane's mother is what's wrong with Jane's mother.
Jane is a very attractive woman, says her mother,

by which she means *I need to lose ten pounds*. Jane needs
to lose ten needs: the need to disprove,

the need to need, the need to disapprove,
the need to use the dusty treadmill in her mother's basement.

The necklace, like all jewelry, is meant to mean. It means
that Jane is Jane's mother's daughter. (The need

to claim.) The necklace is faceted, like a concession.
The necklace is red, like a confession.

Wear the necklace, Jane, Jane thinks.
In the kitchen Jane's mother will be

waiting. The need to hide, the need to be seen.
The need to hide the need to be seen. *There you are*,

her mother will say. The need to be right,
the need to repeat. Jane's mother is right:

Jane should wear more color.

THE PEDESTAL

I wore a white leotard in that part,
which is the most exposed
that you can get, a white
leotard and nothing
else. And then there
was the short, tight,
fluffy, white tutu,
enhancing everything
and hiding nothing,
the white flowered
bikini top and bottom.
He dressed me in
white for twenty years.
I realized that I could
leave the stage only on
the stage. The curtain
rose again and again,
and I was showered
with white roses. He
had so often sent me
white roses. I stood in
my white satin gown
on the center of the stage.
I also wore a pair of long white gloves.

CARTE BLANCHE

The Light and Space Artist has a real crisis on his hands.

The Light and Space Artist is dressed like a rancher.

His belt buckle gleams in sunlight that streams through the slit in the gallery ceiling.

The slit was cut at the Light and Space Artist's request.

The windows of the gallery are papered over.

The corners have been erased.

The white walls have been whitened.

The crisis is the floor.

My job is to make what I make, says the Light and Space Artist.

He makes absence, which is to say perfection.

Which is expensive.

He's been given carte blanche.

The Light and Space Artist flies a 1978 Cessna.

He stockpiles tubes of neon in discontinued colors.

He was born in a town called Globe.

The white of the Light and Space Artist's hair is not the white he uses to dematerialize space or the white of the booties we'll be required to wear to experience his immaculate void.

Voids have matter, he says. I can see the matter.

He sees it when he pilots through cloudless air.

The Light and Space Artist's hair falls in white waves to his shoulders.

Elegant, write the journalists. Well-kept.

A GUIDE TO JANE'S OFFICE

That is a painting of a desolate farmhouse.

That is a children's book about a girl named Jane who paints the sea.

Those are xeroxed pages from a book about female creativity in the Weimar Republic.

Here is the spelling homework that asks, "How old is the <u>sauce</u>? When is my <u>horse</u> coming? Can I go <u>twice</u>?"

What is wrong with the printer?

This is the sunshine on the floor.

This is a website that sells roasted figs at the holidays.

That is the registration form for Intermediate Obedience.

That's a photograph.

That's a photograph.

That's a wooden doll and inside it are smaller dolls.

Each page in that stack says ERROR: undefined.

That's an index card with a quote from Morisot's letters.

That quote is about Morisot's husband being in a bad mood whenever her hair is in disorder.

That's inherited.

This is supposed to help with insomnia.

That space heater is probably dangerous.

That's from the gift shop at the Matisse Chapel.

This coaster hides a water ring.

Here is the bulletin board, empty as a well.

That's trash.

That's recycling.

This stuff needs to be shredded.

That under there is lost.

This is not quite what she expected, though it's possible she never expected.

That sheet of paper says wine
                    compost
                    Dr. Wu?

Here is the thing about female sculptors in the Weimar Republic: their work was celebrated only if it was small.

There is the squirrel staring in from the box gutter.

There is a long thin crack in the wall.

That's nothing.

That's private.

That's due.

JANE IN THE PASSENGER SEAT

The floorboards are wet. The heater is gusting. The sky
is low; the fields blank. You'll have to
ask Dad that, Jane answers. The backseat does not
ask Dad that. It is February in New England.
The destination is Trader Joe's.

Jane knows that centuries ago women crossed fields
to deliver their neighbors' children. They wore snowshoes,
brought honey, rum, and butter. The snow
was stirred like their skirts. The snow
was crusted like sleep. The snow

was deep. (The heat *is* on, Jane tells the backseat.)
As the sky was low, the night was sudden.
The sun, like desire, had occurred.
Jane thinks of wool cloaks congregating on pegs
while the women attended travail. It was *hard*,

it was *very hard & dangerous*. The mother
was *under very Dangerous Circumstances*,
as God intended. Big house little house back house barn,
Jane chants to no one. She will forget
the pickles. She will remember butter

and honey. She will see her husband
standing by a cardboard cupid,
hands in the pockets of his dirty coat,
staring at nothing. *Soon*, she tells the backseat,
which is nearly true.

After a night, or several, a woman emerged
with news. *My wife was Delivered,*
a man recorded. His life—his work—
resumed. The fields needed paths.
The animals needed hay. The snow, the wind, the cold—

nothing abated. A passenger's job is to help.
Sometimes a passenger can't help
but ask the driver what's wrong.

DIAGNOSIS: JANE

- ☑ Not quite ready for a farmshare

- ☑ Overreacts to flowers

- ☑ Spends birthday candle wishes on others

- ☑ Stands still, holding doorknob

- ☑ Keeps earplugs in porcelain dish

- ☑ Mumbles hymns

- ☑ Suggests the fiber farm

- ☑ Suggests maybe an orchard

- ☑ Thinks not infrequently of the scene in which Mrs. Ramsay allows Rose to choose her shawl

- ☑ Blows yet another eyelash from her keyboard

- ☑ Just would never drink milk from the container

- ☑ Has the warranty in her files

- ☑ Knows where the yarn is

- ☑ Knows how to French braid

- ☑ Would really like some help with this duvet cover

- ☑ No, won't be lonely if her daughter goes upstairs to read to her doll

JANE ALONE

—except when did Jane ever *have* her mother and how could she forget the ball turret gunner was a *gunner* and did she really just fake an orgasm to *herself*?

THE OBSTETRICIAN'S LESSON

Woman; Her Diseases and Remedies, 1851

Study the nature of woman, young gentlemen.

A woman is a needling and thimbling machine. She is a menstruous creature. What does she want with algebra? Walter Scott will never do her any harm. The female is naturally prone to be religious. Her pelvis is broad and shallow. The exterior surface of the labia is skin covered with hair. The clitoris is an organ that juts its point forth. Who wants to know, or ought to know that the ladies have abdomens and wombs but us doctors? I beg you to be aware that the womb was never designed to be skewered. Fear is. The lancet is. Puerperal fever is. (You might be disposed to ask why it is.) Barrenness is. To suffer an abortion is. The right breast is. The left one. The whole mass of the nipple itself. You will find a fruitful source of trouble to the female. She has a head almost too small for intellect, but just big enough for love. Her voice. Her susceptible soul. Her inability. As for her beauty. And the sweet sounds of her singing! What do we owe her? What could you do to give the uterus a kindlier disposition? A woman's womb aches. I do not like to see a woman delivered of her child too easily. Inducement is. The hot iron is. Blood-letting is. My hand. The speculum. Perversion is. I assure you that it is.

Gentlemen, do you ask me what is the use of all these remarks? A man's perceptions are his perceptions, and they are what he is.

The womb is

a cul-de-sac

THE DOLL IN THE CONVENT

The convent is stone:
the casket is glass:
the cradle is wood:
the baby is wax.
The gown is satin,
hemmed with lace.
The thread is gold,
the satin pink.
The arms are too long,
the feet correct.
The hair is hair,
a nun's. Perhaps
a novice fastened
the gown and another
lay the baby
down. (Novices
required small
consolations.)

WARP AND WEFT

Augusta Ann Phillips stitched a two-story brick house with two chimneys and five windows.

According to the Division of Home and Community Life, nothing is known about the life of Augusta Ann Phillips.

It is not clear why, in the space after her block uppercase alphabet, Nancy Batchelder stitched *NSABCDMHW*.

Nothing is known about the life of Nancy Batchelder.

Though nothing is known about the life of Maria Minton, we know she knew at least four kinds of stiches: cross, long-armed cross, herringbone, and queen.

Nancy Mary Lindley, about whose life nothing is known, was just eight years old when she stitched
Let virtue be my greatest care
* And study my delight*
So shall my day be always fair
* And peaceable my night.*

Nancy Mary Lindley, we know, learned her alphabet and learned to sit still.

Nothing is known about the life of Lydia Marden, who stitched the gravestone of Sarah Pervier, who died at eight months.

One of Lydia Marden's stitches was detached chain.

From the inscriptions on Mary Shields' sampler, we know she was taught the virtues of piety, prudence, and gratitude. From the source of the inscription on Mary Bishop's sampler—*The Romance of the Forest*—we may surmise she had a taste for the gothic.

Nothing is known about the lives of Mary Shields and Mary Bishop.

Much is known about the life of Tennyson, who wrote
Oh! teach the orphan-boy to read,
Or teach the orphan-girl to sew

It is likely that M. A. Hofman stitched her sampler under the tutelage of Miss Fanny Webber at School No. 7 in Carlisle, Pennsylvania.

M. A. Hofman has not yet been identified.

The Brontë sisters stiched samplers under the tutelage of their Aunt Branwell. (Emily's were neatest.)

Aunt Branwell kept the girls sewing "with purpose or without," believing the activity to be both salutary and proper.

Sewing provides cover, the Brontës knew, for a sewing girl to think. "The most downcast glance," wrote Charlotte, "has its loophole."

Although nothing certain is known about the life of Elizabeth Mason, we know that while sewing deer on green hillocks she was not always thinking of scene or stitch.

Of what did Hannah Hall think while she stitched the two small dogs that might stand for fidelity and watchfulness?

Perhaps her life, about which nothing is known.

QUESTIONS ON JANE'S BIRTHDAY

Is her ring finger really her weakest?

Who put Barbie in the bathroom drawer?

Is it true she remembers every one of her mother's insults?

If so, are they relatively few?

To whom is she praying when she prays to her children?

Will she share with them the raspberries she's hidden?

Is her inability to pretend a fault or a virtue?

How long is forty-four years?

MARY'S YEAR

Mary L. Bowers's Pocket Diary, 1870

Wait

A week seems longer now
than a fortnight used to. I hardly know
what has happened
worthy of recording. I wonder
if he rode up the mountain last night.
I wonder if he is sleepy.
I know him too well to think
that any avoidable circumstance
kept him away. I have no reason
to doubt what he says.
He said he would see me.
Alice Dowd came to see me.
Mr. Clark came to see me.
I have been washing
and got so terrible powerful
that I broke my mop handle
right in two.

Want

Mother went up to Uncle Jacob's
this morning and left me
once more a mistress
of this house. Paulina went up

to play on the melodeon.
To make the cup of my sorrow full,
I must break my watch.
I thought someone would come after me

but no one came.
I mixed up some cake.
I worked on my tidy.
I washed a little

and ironed. Felt as if I didn't care
what became of the work
or me either. Felt as if
I should like to go to bed.

Uncle Fenton must poke down
just at dark with an old frock
for me to patch. I seem to live
without any object.

Wealth

Had a present of some green knit gloves
Had a declamation entitled our glorious dead

Had visitors
Had griddle cakes

Had a nap which refreshed me muchly

Had a gay time, a nice time
Had a firstrate time and good deal of fun over my curls

Had plenty of time to think
and build air castles for the future

Had visitors, had shortcake
(Had rather be alone)

Had a letter from Elnora
Had a letter from Elvira

Mr. L. gave me a cucumber
Mr. Richardson sent me a book

Had strange thoughts and feelings
Sherman sent me an orange

Had some music,
Had a "love feast," a jubilee

Paulina picked a milk pan full of strawberries
and we ate them all up

Had onions for dinner
Had lots of fun by the brook

Had a stove apple in the eve
and that was more than I expected

Weather

Rainy in the forenoon but pleasant in the afternoon.
Pleasant in the afternoon but cloudy in the morning.
Pleasant, a beautiful day for our picnic. Pleasant
but I did not wash. Rainy this forenoon but pleasant
this afternoon. Pleasant part of the day but showery
a little. Pleasant. Have felt about used up today +
consequently rather blue. Pleasant. I believe it has been
the hottest day I ever knew. Pleasant and excessively
warm. Another very pleasant day. Pleasant—I washed.
Rainy in the morn but pleasant in the afternoon. Pleasant
in the morning but clouded up and rained by noon.
Rainy in the forenoon but pleasant in the afternoon
and I am still at Mr. Palmer's waiting for someone
to come after me. Pleasant and cool. Pleasant but
windy and cold. Cold, cloudy, windy and squally.
I guess there will be pleasant days after this.

Weight

I have a heavy weight
I dare not tell

I would like to tell

Ellen's weight 152
George's 134 ½
Melissa's 130, and mine 132

Mother came down through the snow
to see how I was

I went up stairs before dark

Welcome

The covenant meeting, the prayer meeting, the class meeting, the female prayer meeting, the evening meeting, the Library Association's meeting, campmeeting, the Springfield campmeeting, the five o'clock meeting, aftermeeting, some future meeting, the town meeting . . . .

Welfare

F. S. Henry 21 years old today.
Collins Pomeroy 23 years old today.
Arthur Gain's 9 today.
J. F. Northnay 60 years old today.

Mrs. Mary Eggleston had a little daughter
born Tuesday. Mrs. Beckwith had a little daughter
born last week Tuesday.
It is quite pretty for one so small.

Helen Crosby died last night
from the effects of burns received Thursday.
Mr. Goodrich Moore was buried
in Granville today. Died yesterday.

Eddie is sick with typhoid fever.

Lamira B. 21 years old today.
Abie Henry 18 years old today.
Paulina is 14 years old today,
the dear child.

Welter

If he only was—
If he only would become—
My own dear precious one

I made ready
I made ready

But he don't want to come

(I can not blame anyone)

My faithful or faithless friend

Wherewithal

I sewed on Paula's pink dress. I fixed
      Paulina's white dress.
            I ripped up and ironed

Jane's old black silk dress. If there is
      any such thing
            as "<u>perfect</u>" love

or perfection in holiness, I want to know it.
      I am sure I have
            never known it yet.

I trimmed over my old hat and fixed it
      for my best one.
            I sewed on

my purple dress the afternoon some,
      but ate peaches
            most of the time.

I've cried more than before in six weeks
      but—after all
            what is the use!

I cut out an overskirt of that black silk
      that used to be
            Jane's dress.

Will

....
....
....
....
....
....
....
....
....
.... but I done up
a bundle of letters
with his watch—ring—
and sleeve buttons
to return to him

and then sat down
to have a cry over it.

                Oh!

Wisdom

1. Harden not your heart
2. Lord increase our faith
3. "Beautiful": yes that is the word "beautiful"
4. Here if anywhere one has need of patience
5. ½ lb. of Butternut bark / ¼ lb. yellow dock root / ¼ lb. of licorice /
   1 oz of saffron / 1 oz of Anise seed
6. I am certain of nothing
7. In this world there is always some little thing to prevent our happiness
   from being complete
8. This may grow brighter + brighter

Wishes

Mrs. Gilmore, Mrs. Singer, Mrs. Andrus, Mrs. Palmer . . . .
I made calls all day.

Mrs. P. is about sick with a cold.
Mrs. S. had one of her peculiar streaks.
Mrs. L. was full of trouble
and kinder cross.

Mrs. G. is a queer woman. I have an impression
that she don't like me + for that reason
I don't like her.

It is six weeks today
since George and Melissa were married.

I sometimes think I wish—
I do so much wish—
I do wish I ever could—

It is useless to talk wish.

I thought Mrs. Kellogg had neuralgia in her shoulder
and I made some bread for her.

Witnesses

We all went to church and in a sleigh ride
for the first time this winter.
The wind blew and snow fell.
The snow is drifted quite badly in some places
but we all went. I think every member
of the church was present.
The church voted.
For the good of the church
and the unconverted around us. Six rose
for prayers. It kept on
snowing. Mr. Humphrey preached. The praying
band from Westfield were there.
We reorganize the S School next Sunday
and open the contribution box
and have a jubilee. "Ye will not come
to me that ye might have life." I came home
feeling I can't tell how.

Woe

I loved him and now I can not forget him I love him as well as ever I am determined to give him up but

44

Words

Mary came up here and pitched into me
rough shod but I bore it patiently.
Uncle Jacob made me quite a visit
and tried to find out about my affairs.
I think if I was in Julia's place I should
take some of the plain hints given me
about long visits. Edd Loomis came up
and gave me a lecture. I wish everyone
would just mind their own business
and let mine alone. Mr. Doolittle preached
from the same text
                    all
                        day

Work

I washed. I ironed. I quilted. I
made bread. I made seven pies
and rye bread. I made rye bread
and 6 pumpkin pies. I cleaned
the west chamber. I cleaned the
north chamber. John William
and I put down the carpet in
the parlor. Mother came down
and we cut up and packed
down two hams. I washed. I
ironed. I baked bread and pies.
I washed a little in the
forenoon, made bread—
doughnuts +c. I made a cream
pie. I made a shortcake. Mother
made candles and we was all
cross. I washed butter cloths. I
washed the parlor curtains. I
washed dishes, butter boxes,
and clothes. I made 9 pies. I
sewed. We washed and I don't
know what else. I churned,
made bread, tried calves tallow,
+ c + c. I quilted as a matter
of course. I washed. I ironed. I
sewed. I washed out my
clothes. I blacked the parlor
stove. Then I washed my feet
and went to bed.

World

Down into the pasture
To "Mother Palmer's"
Out on to the pond

To the southlane
To Southwick
To town

Up to Grandmother's
Up to witness the opening of the sabbath school box
Up to see Alice according to agreement

To the dedication of the Masonic hall
To see the fireworks
Up to the corner to get the mail

To the Library Association,
the question for discussion was
"Resolved that capital punishment should be abolished from the United States"

To be gone
To be entertained
To be wholly

released
To hear Miss Olympia Brown from Bridgeport
To hear Mr. Marsh (the colored minister) preach

After huckleberries but did not get many
After the cows but couldn't find them all
After young winter greens with the Warren children

After birch
I think this is not so bad a world
after all

After all that has been
said and done
I sat in the door and heard the Granville band play

Worth

Another New Year I am spared to see.
The future I do not dare try
to picture before me.

I know something more
than I knew before.

I am full of wonderments.

JANE IN THE INTERLUDE

In not so many words, Jane is thinking

of the *irreligious snow*
and the *close and holy darkness*.

"Let's sing Christmas songs," says her daughter.
"I'll go first."

JANE AND THE ESCAPES

Jane reads about an octopus that slipped through a gap at the top of its tank, slithered eight feet across the floor, then slid one hundred sixty-four feet down a drainpipe into the sea.

Jane's friend tells her that her favorite disorder is dissociative fugue.

The sign on Jane's daughters' fort says Jane can come in, but Jane does not.

How is Jane? She's Jane.

It was futile to argue with Jane's father, and it is still is.

Jane's husband says, "It doesn't concern you."

Where is Jane going? She'll be right back.

What is she doing? She'll be right back.

The morning staff found a wet trail across the aquarium floor.

"We'll miss him, but we hope he does well in his new life," said the aquarium manager.

There's always Thoreau's rsvp: "*such are my engagements to myself,* that I dare not promise."

The only inflexible part of an octopus is its beak.

At night, Jane reads to her daughters about a donkey that becomes a rock.

Don't worry, Jane stays Jane.

The way Earth looked from orbit, said the astronaut.

Jane's daughters spinning on the lawn.

The octopus that escaped had a name and so did the one that stayed.

A CONCEPT OF SERVICE

Mr. B[alanchine]. There are a lot of horses in the U.S. and when you choose them to run, some are faster and better.

Dancer. He gave us red horse blankets, each embroidered with a sobriquet. I didn't lose my job, but I did lose my name.

Mr. B. The bodies are ready for anything, we use them faster.

Dancer. Speedy-foot Gelso. Kentucky Cookie. Mandago Pie. All the good solid things he used as comparisons.

Mr. B. Exceptional bodies. Legs and hands that are ready to move in any direction at any speed at any time. When they come to me they don't know anything and I teach them.

Dancer. Your legs change, your body changes, you become a filly. I wasn't used to working like that, and my feet would bleed.

Mr. B. They develop speed and grace. They are obedient. You say count to 175 and they will count to 175. Then you can say thank you, now go home.

Dancer. Some people are good with untamed animals. They don't startle the creatures.

Mr. B. I don't think lots, I just manipulate. I am the audience, the judge.

Dancer. He would be the only judge, relieving me of having to criticize myself.

Mr. B. I like to look at them and show how they look and move.

Dancer. Nobody ever really answered my questions.

Mr. B.

Dancer. You have to give up some fantasies about yourself.

Mr. B.

Dancer. This is a sophisticated concept of service.

Mr. B. I like to live now, today. What will be 10 years from now, 100 years, who cares?

Dancer. It's inevitable that someone will replace you.

Mr. B. My days are the same routine. Pouring water into the sieve.

EXAMPLES OF THE DECLARATIVE
IN JANE'S KITCHEN

You're not being a good person like Ghandi.

I can see the sides of your head pumping while you chew.

I don't want *my mind taken off of it.*

I was going to do it but then I didn't.

I'm counting to a thousand.

I'm raking my own damn leaves.

Questioning is how we learn, Dad.

Sometimes I laugh so hard the sound of my laughter goes away.

LIFE-SIZED PORTRAIT

Jean-Michel has found Suzanne like a small box. He calls her Venus. Come and give me a bath, Venus, he says. Venus, read me the names of the bones in an arm. Hey, Venus, come and kiss me. Venus, go get us some coke.

Jean-Michel sucks Suzanne's fingers.

There are no black men in museums, Jean-Michel says. Try counting. Jean-Michel disappears for weeks.

Jean-Michel likes to spit into Suzanne's mouth. Beautiful arms, he says. Venus, I have to paint your arms. Jean-Michel lets Suzanne brush his teeth. Don't talk to me, Venus, he says. I hate your Canadian accent.

Jean-Michel says, Burroughs was a junkie, Parker was a junkie. It is the road to genius. Do you want some money, Venus?

Jean-Michel puts on a Charlie Parker tape and tells Suzanne to be very quiet. He is afraid the KKK is going to kill him because he is getting so famous and he is black.

(Let me give you a bath, Suzanne says. You always like that.)

Jean-Michel tells Suzanne to lie down on a canvas that is on the floor. He fills in the life-sized portrait. He kisses the face in the drawing but he does not kiss Suzanne.

Jean-Michel says, Why have you left me, Venus? Everyone has left me. He tells her to open her hand and spits into her palm.

EXAMPLES OF THE IMPERATIVE
IN JANE'S KITCHEN

Don't take it out on me.

Don't take it out on us.

Don't take it out on them.

Don't get all Lady Macbeth.

Have a banana.

THE BALLET MASTER

if you are lucky you still feel
him inside you are attuned
to what you know he wanted
dancers are like nuns they say
and in a way we were
the instruments of his creative powers
believe as we did and you are not
yourself any longer
where do you go from him
there was no comprehending
what he felt or thought he could
mold from you anything
he wanted *I know where you were*
I know what you ate I know
where you slept he was our conscience
the most exciting relationship
was with him his hands
on our necks our legs our backs what
would he do next
everyone was watching
dancers are like wine sweet
before they ripen
then vinegar he said old dancers
they should just go away
and die we didn't have to speak
he saw what was inside us
it might be enough to live
a whole life on if you are lucky
you still feel him inside you my place is
with ghosts he said I'm not old
I've just lived a long time

THE VOCATION OF SAINT THÉRÈSE

I look upon myself as a *weak little bird,*
with only a light down as covering.
The little bird wills *to fly* toward the bright Sun
that attracts its eye, imitating its brothers.
But alas! the only thing it can do is *raise its little wings*
To fly is not within its *little* power!
What then will become of it? Will it die of sorrow
at seeing itself so weak? Oh no!
the little bird will not even be troubled.
The little bird will not change its place.
At times the little bird's heart is assailed
by the storm. This is the moment of *perfect joy*
for the *poor little weak creature*
I can understand Your love for the little bird
because it has not strayed far from You.
The little bird turns toward its beloved Sun,
presenting its wet wings.

Deleted: I would want to die on the field of battle

Deleted: I would want to preach

Deleted: I would like to travel over the whole earth to preach

Deleted: And with what love would I give You to souls!

Deleted: I would shed my blood for You even to the very last drop

Deleted: I would be scourged and crucified

Deleted: I would die flayed

Deleted: I would be plunged into boiling oil

Deleted: I would undergo all the tortures

Deleted: I would present my neck to the sword

Deleted: I would whisper at the stake Your Name

BASIC READER

WORD LIST

1	10	19	29
Dick	here	he	guess
see	I	20	30
run	am	something	fun
2	11	play	will
Jane	where	21	31
3	is	find	you
Baby	not	the	32
4	12	ball	saw
said	oh	22	in
Mother	13	it	33
Father	look	jump	rabbit
5	14	23	pretty
come	laughed	good-by	34
and	a	away	thank
6	funny	24	35
what	15	make	----------
can	Spot	dog	36
7	Little	25	grandmother
to	Mew	she	happy
dinner	16	kitten	37
8	want	26	candy
one	17	house	38
two	bow-wow	big	cookies
three	18	27	39
9	some	went	----------
ran	this	28	
they		how	

A SMALL MOVEMENT OF FREEDOM INSIDE OF FATE

Ask the fox about her workday and she'll tell you about a massacre in 13th-century France.

Ask the fox about the sufficiency of love and she'll tell you she's always thinking of the big bang.

Like all foxes, the fox is wary.

She sits at the edge of her floral sofa.

She does not unclasp her hands.

The fox can see the expressions beneath our expressions.

She hears the silence beneath our noise.

In her deep and husky voice, the fox says *primitive*: "We're such primitive creatures." She says *nature*: Her mother "did what her nature prescribed."

Ask the fox about her novels and she'll tell you she finds geology so aesthetically and metaphorically pleasing—these great events in the earth in turmoil.

The fox knows turmoil.

Her third husband says her father was worse than her mother.

Though old, the fox is agile.

You've got to pick up your bed and walk, she says.

She knows life is impersonal.

No, the fox has never had any female role models.

No, she cannot feel herself part of any group.

Once upon a time the fox worked for a magician.

Once upon a time she drove a crane.

Once upon a time she made "quick intense love in dark courtyards" with a Corsican politician.

Once upon a time she felt she had to say yes to men, and women too.

Truth, that's what I care about, says the fox, who learned the necessity of judgment.

The fox's home has many exits.

She knows she's just passing through.

JANE AND THE VISITORS

A mouse. In a dark drawer
it shreds the bristles of a basting brush,
gleaning oil from the boar's hair,
then rears, snout stained
by a bouillon cube.
Far far away, Jane lies
in white noise; her dreams, if remembered,
will surprise
then confirm. Her daughters' legs lengthen
like the mouse's incisors
that crumble the golden cube—
nownownownownow
goes its creature heart. And now and now and now
go the hearts upstairs, each one
bigger than a mouse. Each heart
has four rooms and each room
has a door. Jane's drawer
holds an heirloom ring, a lock of hair,
and a box of teeth.
The mouse shreds, the family
sleeps, a hand slips a coin
beneath a pillow. She can't
be real, a girl thinks,
a fairy winging through the night
with a bag of teeth.

The light assembles, the birds
discuss. The coin
is there, the mouse

is gone.

JANE'S SOUVENIR

. . . and then, through a window, Jane saw a fox.
Saw a fox and thought, Foxes are small.
The fox was a dash, a vanishing

fact. You only see a fox.
You only have seen it. Jane at dawn
with a small thought

and a tube of biscuits.

MATISSE'S GREAT-GRANDDAUGHTER, OR JANE AND THE LONG WAY

1.

I begin where

1.

Here, at a good desk, in adequate light.

I begin again at the website of the artist Sophie Matisse, Henri's great-granddaughter.

Her paintings are replicas of famous paintings from which she removes all living figures.

The bather from *The Valpinçon Bather.*
The lacemaker from *The Lacemaker*.
Woman with a pearl necklace from *Woman with a Pearl Necklace.*
The dancers from *The Dance Class*.

Click, click.

1.

The goldfish from Sophie's great-grandfather's *Goldfish*.

I misremember how many. (It's four, not three.)

I contemplate absent presences and present absences.

Perhaps I just think about them.

"Cyclamen," I begin.

"[E]merald."

"[F]ocal points."

Matisse said he wouldn't mind turning into a vermillion goldfish, which I quote.

Picasso said Matisse had the sun in his gut, which I don't.

Why are goldfish orange, I ask the search engine.

If left in the dark, they can become almost gray.

1.

I begin where Sophie did, with the *Mona Lisa*.

What if, Sophie thought, looking at a book of variations on da Vinci's painting—nude Mona Lisa, fat Mona Lisa, Mona Lisa with a mustache—she just got up and left?

Sophie hadn't painted for years; her daughter was four.

In parentheses I quote Matisse on the work/life balance.

No, I won't quote Matisse on the work/life balance.

(Will I ever get to quote Matisse on the work/life balance?)

1.

I begin where Sophie did, with a book of variations on the *Mona Lisa*.

Blonde Mona Lisa, zombie Mona Lisa, llama Mona Lisa. Poor woman, Sophie thought. She's had enough done to her.

Having not painted for years, Sophie resumed: the balustrade, the landscape behind Mona Lisa.

Is there a *behind* Mona Lisa? Was there?

A Renaissance sky, bluffs, a river . . . .

One could suppose that the landscape doesn't exist, said the chief curator of European paintings at the Louvre, that it is the young woman's own dream world.

Da Vinci made that young woman a da Vinci. What did Sophie do to her? Or for her.

I write her name, check the spelling.

1.

I begin in the "wonderful old French farmhouse in Villiers-sous-Grez." In the living room, where the Matisse family has gathered.

I can't stand the idea of an artist named Sophie Matisse, says Sophie's step-grandmother. If it doesn't work, she can always try a new name later, says her grandfather. She'll be happier without people always comparing her to Matisse, says her father.

Sophie, engaged to be married, listens. Beautiful Sophie, whose neckline is, I imagine, generous; Dyslexic Sophie, who failed out of the art school where her great-grandfather studied.

Beautiful Dyslexic Sophie, about to marry a man twice her age.

As did Mona Lisa, I recall.

Married Sophie will later claim that, as she listened to her family decide whether or not she would change her name, she "*seemed* to have no opinion of [her] own" (emphasis mine).

Matisse: a hissing iamb.

(Reader, she kept it.)

1.

What does a descendent of Matisse who paints paint?

Pronounced statements of absence, said the critic.

Conceptual art, with lots of frosting, said Sophie.

1.

I attempt chronology: Sophie drops out of college and moves to France and enrolls in L'École des Beaux-Arts where her great-grandfather studied and has an open account at Lefebvre-Foinet and the other students are jealous and Sophie withdraws to her room and dresses in tatters and is committed to painting but doesn't dare say so and is slow to learn French because she is dyslexic and is asked to leave the Beaux-Arts but by that time has met her future husband . . . .

1.

What *can* a descendent of Matisse who paints paint?

I could begin in the corner of an exhibit in Baltimore where Matisse's daughter's paintings hang—one landscape, one still life. Worried that her signature would be mistaken for his, she destroyed most others. But I don't want to write about Marguerite Matisse's devotion to her father and I don't have to.

I was like his wife, she said.

1.

Matisse with panic attacks, Matisse with insomnia, Matisse at work from morning to dusk
Matisse with palpitations, with a constant drumming in his ears
Matisse ordering oysters to paint, not eat

Matisse in a suit, Matisse in a long white coat
Matisse's reminder that the foot is a bridge
Matisse in his aviary, Matisse with his violin
Matisse on a ladder, Matisse holding scissors
Matisse's routine, his simple supper
That photograph of Matisse clutching a white pigeon
Matisse swearing under his breath as he worked
Matisse drawing on the ceiling with a piece of charcoal affixed to a stick of bamboo

Matisse staring at a nude model
searching for the door that he must break down
to reach the garden
in which he is *so alone*
and so happy

Matisse as black hole, Matisse as sun

The gravity of Matisse

I wait to begin

1.

After Sophie painted *Goldfish* without the fish, she painted Matisse's *The Conversation* without the conversing couple: Matisse and his wife.

I begin there. With the empty chair that held Madame Matisse in her long black gown, Madame Matisse who said, As for me, I'm in my element when the house burns down.

Who married the person who told her, I love you dearly, mademoiselle; but I shall always love painting more.

Who felt indispensable. (Matisse knew how to make people feel that way, said the woman who replaced her.)

1.

I begin in the Louvre, where Matisse copied the old masters.

Raphael, Poussin, Chardin . . . .

Only the cowardly would avoid them.

For six years he painted Chardin's *The Skate*. Magisterial, said a fellow student. At once a Chardin and a Matisse.

No—I begin in the Louvre, where the female relations of the museum guards painted replicas to sell to the Purchasing Commission.

It had to be a servile copy, said Matisse, not an intelligent one.

The mothers, wives, and daughters of the museum guards—
they didn't use a magnifying glass;
they didn't obsess over texture and glaze;
they didn't lose days in the study of blue.

Matisse was broke but he couldn't be as literal as the women.

They copied best, he said.

1.

I begin with that edition of *Jazz* beneath young Sophie's pillow.

She liked the sword swallower best. She thought it was a rabbit with three ears.

I'm staring at it when my twelve-year-old comes in. What do you need, I ask. What's that, she says.

Lately she's been painting. Always solitary girls, always from behind because she can't do faces.

They wear dresses, stand before seas and fields, beneath big skies. Their hair hangs long, concealing and revealing their need to reveal and conceal.

What does it look like to you, I ask.

A person puking stuff into the air, she says.

1.

I begin with what's there.

With what was already there.

With what was never there.

The balustrade in *Mona Lisa*.
The porch in *American Gothic*.
The indented bedding in *The Bather*.

That southwestern portion of the map of the Low Countries in *The Art of Painting*.

Shadows, mirrors, and walls.

I'm squinting at my screen, trying to read the poster in Sophie's *The Dance Lesson*, when a bird flies into my window.

It lies dying for five minutes then flies away.

1.

I wish

Sophie did not

Subtitle her Mona Lisa "Be Back in 5 Minutes"
Exhibit the painting in a bank vault
Wear a "sexy, scoop-neck green top" to the interview
Design limited edition luxury items

Or say "fun" so often:

That was the most fun. Life is too short not to have some fun. Learning a new language is fun. It was fun to do, a quick painting . . . .

I wish Sophie and her art didn't make me wish so much.

What does a descendant of Matisse who paints paint?

It was Sophie's husband's idea that she paint the *Mona Lisa* without Mona Lisa, and I wish it weren't.

They sat looking at the book of variations: Mona Lisa with a pipe; in a bowler; on a dollar. She should just get up and leave, said Sophie.

You could paint that, said her husband.

1.

And I wish the art critic didn't write that Sophie "had just stepped out of a Renoir."

Sophie sat beside him in a *garden swing* at her dealer's *Yorktown Heights estate* over *Memorial Day weekend* looking at *a catalog of her Tokyo show*, pointing out *the fineness of her own brushstrokes.*

She was trapped, he decided. A beautiful trapped woman, whom he would, he wrote, liberate through interpretation.

Men act, says John Berger. Women appear.

On her website Sophie appears nineteen times: as a child, as a bride, *with the Prince of Monaco*, on a terrace in *Saint-Jean-Cap-Ferrat* wearing *pearls . . . .*

That garden swing, that terrace, those photo shoots with *Vogue, Madame, Style St Barth*—what if she just got up and left?

1.

I begin at the Beaux-Arts where Sophie, a gifted copyist, learns she can't draw. A Matisse would instinctively know how, she'd thought.

She sits in life drawing class, as exposed as the model.

She nods, pretending to understand French.

If he could bring the model inside him, Matisse said, he could improvise, let his hand run free. Only by identifying with his subjects could he get free of his emotions.

Sophie says she felt free—"completely free"—when she erased the subjects of famous paintings.

In life drawing class a beautiful young woman sits before a beautiful young woman.

I discourse upon freedom, authority, transcendence, and female subjectivity.

I quote John Berger.

Nevertheless, it remains that Sophie was a Matisse who didn't know French and couldn't draw.

1.

Why do I begin

to stare at Sophie's chest

in all these photographs that so prominently feature her chest?

A lovely, irrelevant, prominent chest.

What does a female descendant of Matisse who paints wear?

Why must I see Sophie's body

as my problem?

1.

Though I know better I begin with Sophie's self-portrait.

Asked to depict herself, she paints the ghost of a headless nude: the white bedsheet in Courbet's *The Origin of the World*. Her sheet retains, or rather becomes, the infamous form in Courbet's painting:

Breast with erect nipple
Smooth stomach
Spread thighs
Labial folds

Self-portrait as copy. Self-portrait as copy of male painter's provocative female nude. Self-portrait as copy of a male painter's provocative female nude that lacks head, arms, hands, and lower legs. But a copy of a nude in which the nude is removed. But a copy in which the removed nude is evoked in the bright bedsheet. Self-portrait as bedsheet.

I don't know what to say about this. Neither does my husband.

We stare at the painting, looking for Sophie.

Asked to comment, Sophie says, I feel like in this career I've chosen, with the name and the situation that I have, I can't make anything up. I just have to show myself.

She's thirty-eight. She can speak French now, and draw.

1.

I'm forty-eight. My French is rudimentary. My poems have appeared.

I make lists. I list every painting that Sophie altered.

She chose paintings so iconic that viewers would attempt to conjure the original, and thus preoccupied, or so she reasoned, they would not immediately compare her work to her great-grandfather's.

Sophie never once—I double check—selected the work of a female painter.

Then again it occurs to me that there may not be a sufficiently iconic painting by a woman. In the history of art.

I google "iconic paintings by women."

The engine gently corrects my preposition to "of," and provides a list of what it calls Famous Classic Paintings of Women.

Searches related to my search for iconic paintings by women:
famous paintings of women's faces
paintings of women's bodies
famous paintings of women's backs
beautiful woman oil painting
famous painting of woman sitting in chair
beautiful woman painting images
famous paintings of women's bodies
painting of beautiful Indian woman

1.

A page of fragments, each beginning with a subordinating conjunction
A fairy tale called The Princess and the Great Master
Another stab at chronology

Forty footnotes—but at the foot of what?

There's always first person,
I think.

1.

I walk to work like Wallace Stevens. He would have agreed with Matisse that the only real light is that in the artist's mind. Matisse would have agreed with Stevens that description is revelation.

I'm not thinking about that. I'm not thinking about the opulent eye, the lavish imagination. About blossoms and cockatoos and dishes of peaches.

Stevens handed slips of paper to his secretary, but I try the dictation function on my phone. (I've seen Britty do this at my daughter's basketball games.)

I don't know how loudly to speak. I don't know I have to speak my punctuation.

Also, it's windy.

I mutter some lines about the artist Sophie Matisse, but the phone takes liberty, not dictation:

Having that pain and for years so if she
painted he was there and she ran in there
and she left the house and imagined

Such an overwrought device.

I didn't say pain. I wouldn't.

That pain—it must have come from paint.

1.

I begin at Bookland in Sarasota. Home from college with a nascent sense of self and art history, I buy a matted reproduction of Matisse's *Goldfish*.

I don't call my high school friends.

I am, as John Berger says, almost continually accompanied by an image of myself.

My self sees herself stash the print in her closet, like money in an account.

Back at college, I funnel beer. I dress for a formal called Old South, for a party called Pimp and Whore. I stare out the window as my professor recites a sonnet, and look down when he calls the dirty pun "delicious." I survey my own femininity. I like Intro to Art History, its dim auditorium. I like learning in the dark.

1.

I begin at midnight in the old French farmhouse in Villiers-sous-Grez. Everyone is asleep except Sophie and her grandmother Teeny. They've been playing backgammon; now they talk and eat dark chocolate. There's the sound of wind, or the sound of rain, or the sound of an owl, or the sound of a train.

That Teeny is the ex-wife of Pierre Matisse (son of Henri) *and* the widow of Marcel Duchamp;

that a visiting gallerist snores lightly in the guest room;

that earlier he had been permitted to bathe in the blue polyester resin hippopotamus that François-Xavier Lalanne made for Teeny and Marcel;

that it's been said that Teeny "accommodated and complimented Duchamp's genius";

that as a teenager she aspired to be an artist and went to Paris for that purpose;

that she convinced famous male artists to let her make prints of their palms—
Picasso, Miró, Matisse, Chagall, Matta—

that Pierre left Teeny for Matta's young wife;

that in response to this news, Matisse wrote to Pierre, "Watch out! A young woman
has young claws, well sharpened";

(this despite his contemporaneous advertisement for a night nurse stipulating that
she be "young and pretty")—

it doesn't belong here.

Teeny is the one who tells Sophie she's talented. With Teeny, Sophie said, I knew I
would be fine.

The sound of an owl, the sound of a train. The sound of their laughter.

A clock strikes one.

1.

If I begin with the death of Teeny Duchamp—or, rather, with the "small but elegant
homage" to her held at the Jeu de Paume at which were displayed the prints she
made of famous men's palms—can I reach Sophie's hands?

She stares at them, noting how much they resemble her great-grandfather's.

Square fingers, thick and long, with flat nails.

She keeps the nails blue. Matisse blue, she says.

I see them flit like minnows in her daughter's bubble bath.

1.

A salad bowl, porcelain, white. A bowl "decorated with great charm and delicacy in a severely simple pattern of dark blue dots and lines."

Painted by Anna Matisse, Henri's mother. She worked in gouache on porcelain, a respectable hobby. She ran the housepaints section of the family store.

In their drab mill town in the cold, gray North, her glass bottles of color stood like envoys. Cadmium, cobalt, ultramarine . . . .

She bought Matisse his first box of art supplies. He was 20; he'd passed the bar exam; he was ill and confined to bed.

That box of color—I threw myself into it like a beast that plunges towards the thing it loves, he said.

Naturally, his stern father was disappointed.

Not Anna: she loved everything Henri did.

She had, he said, a face with generous features.

Anna kept her big stove permanently lit. She painted porcelain. Drank lime blossom tea.

In the shop, Henri watched her weigh birdseed and fish food on tiny brass scales.

Everything she painted could break, and did.

This bowl, with which I begin, is her last remaining piece.

1.

I could begin with Sophie's ambition: to be an artist, to see her name on a museum wall. To squeeze, as she put it, into art history somehow.

As though art history were a crowded elevator or a sleek gown.

As though her art were her body and her body were wrong.

It's true, women have dimensions, like paintings.

Their big ambitions require small frames.

Somehow.

As for Matisse, he aspired "to invent a new language for painting," said his biographer, speaking from her home in North London.

1.

Where did the Mona Lisa *go*?

Or the lacemaker, the woman with a pearl necklace, the bather.

The dancers, I imagine, went home to wash out their tights and hang them on radiators to dry.

Until I learn they didn't have radiators. Or, in many cases, running water.

They had second jobs.

They had widowed mothers and younger siblings.

They had the attentions of wealthy elderly *abonnés*.

They had a sobriquet: *les petit rats*.

They had, as one Parisian diarist put it, *a world of pink and white*.

They had gilded walls and torn costumes.

They had Degas, his fascination and disgust.

They had class the next morning.

1.

Maybe we shouldn't have skipped the Louvre, I think, staring at *The Lacemaker*.

Like a painter, she is absorbed in her work. Or, as Sir Lawrence Gowing, Commander of the Most Excellent Order of the British Empire, puts it, she is "enclosed in her own lacy world."

Sir Gowing, I recall, organized a major Matisse exhibition.

I lose an hour reading a pdf of the catalog.

I learn that the art *is* the artist. That Matisse, when asked to nurse the ill, would loan them his paintings before leaving to paint.

Also that his "systematic and deliberate self-engrossment" constituted a profound innovation in twentieth-century painting.

Self as gateway to the sublime.

To his "solitary, epoch-making destination."

I blow an eyelash from my keyboard.

1.

We shouldn't have skipped the Louvre.

There on Vermeer's smallest canvas the lacemaker leans like a surgeon over her work.

You can look.

Millions each year do. Peering as through a keyhole

they get close to the painting

but not to her.

Look at that, they whisper.

Pointing to her hands, the impossible thread.

The privacy she makes.

1.

I begin by trying to ignore my daughter's piano scales.

Whole whole half whole whole whole half

The scales are loud, and pretty.

I should listen to these pretty scales

that she doesn't want to be playing

on a Saturday.

Matisse made his son rise early to practice scales alone in the salon.

When the boy fell asleep on the piano bench, the father in his bed upstairs rapped on the floor with a stick.

Pierre was forbidden to play rough games. He wore overly long sleeves to protect his hands.

There he is in *The Piano Lesson*, trapped between a teacher and a metronome. His face is abstract but his sadness is not.

A lit candle keeps time on the lid of the miniature grand.

Outside is the garden and beyond that the muddy trenches of Verdun.

I love my family, truly, dearly, and profoundly, but from a distance, said Matisse.

1.

I begin in another thicket:

That woman behind the boy is, as it turns out, not the piano teacher but the subject of Matisse's painting *Woman on a High Stool*. That is, in *The Piano Lesson*, Matisse painted one of his own paintings. (Sir Gowing is instructive on the increasingly private and self-referential world of Matisse's work.) He did not however reproduce the entire painting; he removed the image of a bird on the wall behind the seated woman. That image of the bird was, it turns out, a drawing by young Pierre. That is, Matisse erased his reproduction of his son's work (sketch of bird) from a reproduction of his own work (*Woman on a High Stool*) in a painting ostensibly about his son (*The Piano Lesson*). Pierre: "He suppressed everything that he did not need—no more drawing by me."

Of *The Piano Lesson*, Pierre said, Well, I wouldn't mind having it.

1.

I begin in a hotel room in Paris. A renowned art dealer turns the pages of Sophie's sketchbook while Sophie watches.

He doesn't speak.

A clock tocks like a metronome.

For his meticulous stewardship of modern European art, the dealer is regarded by some as an artist himself. His gallery bears his name: Pierre Matisse.

Pierre's father never approved of his profession; his father approved, it's true, of little. When, as a boy, Pierre rushed to him with a color he had discovered, Henri looked down and said, You haven't discovered anything.

In the hotel room, Pierre closes the sketchbook. C'est tout? he says.

1.

I begin with the problem of verbs.

In her Missing Persons series, Sophie Matisse _____

    a. erased
    b. liberated
    c. exploited
    d. revealed

Sophie says she felt invisible at the time in her life when she did whatever she did.

            nothing
            Nobody
            why?

she wrote on her calendar—July 11, 1992, a Saturday—in the year before she disappears from the photographic timeline on her website.

Beautiful dyslexic female, age 28, last seen walking through a French village with infant daughter, grandmother Teeny, and a dog named Gauguin.

Eight years later that might be her in the snowy mist near the summit of Machu Picchu.

Meanwhile she's been blanking figures from the frames of great masters.

Leaving, as she says, her invisible mark.

In a studio, a stairwell, a boudoir, a boat . . . .

Conceptual art as self-portrait.

Leaving no trace is the trace she leaves.

1.

I try to remember where I first encountered Sophie's paintings.

I fill out a medical form for summer camp.

The neighbor's dog walks past with a looped leash in its mouth.

I stare at a piece of paper on which I've written *lacy world*.

1.

I begin in the haunted stillness of a child's room without a child in it.

Her strewn clothes look like the victims at Pompeii. A stuffed tiger stares at the wall.

I came in here for *something*.

Now time is visible.

I hover and blink.

1.

My question is simple.

Where did who go, my husband says.

Mona Lisa, I say.

He shrugs. How would he know?

Magic Mona Lisa, missing Mona Lisa, Mona Lisa absent without leave.

Mona Lisa on the lam.

With some dancers.

And a lacemaker.

A woman with a pearl necklace.

And a bather.

In her robe.

With a pitchfork.

And a bag of fish.

Four, not three.

Don't forget the headless nude.

Or her copy of *Ways of Seeing*.

Sophie's driving.

Is she?

There's a pack of cigarettes on the dash.

Gauloises. No—Virginia Slims.

Virginia Slims.

You've come a long way, baby.

38.

I've come the long way.

Back to my grandmother's house, her cluttered condo.

Nine and bored

cross-legged on the floor

with a stack of magazines and a pair of scissors.

I'm cutting out women

from cigarette ads.

Western, equestrian, nautical, disco.

In knee socks, jumpsuits, pearls, fur.

Rompers, roller skates, gold lamé.

And their hair!

The scissors are dull, but I'm a diligent girl.

I arrange the figures on the braided rag rug

and then arrange them again

and again.

My menagerie.

My grandmother.

Oh there you are, Jane, she says.

NOTES

"Einstein's Dinner": The main source of the information in this poem is *The Uncommon Vision of Sergei Konenkov, 1874–1971: A Russian Sculptor and His Times*, edited by Marie Turbow Lampard, John E. Bowlt, and Wendy R. Salmond.

"Seven Students": The text in this poem is from interviews in the *Paris Review* with Elizabeth Hardwick, Toni Morrison, Janet Malcolm, Joan Didion, Joy Williams, Ann Beattie, and Deborah Eisenberg.

"The Pedestal": The text in this poem is from statements made by Diana Adams, Suzanne Farrell, and Allegra Kent.

"Carte Blanche": This poem sometimes quotes or paraphrases Doug Wheeler.

"Jane in the Passenger Seat": The italicized portions of this poem are from the family record of Dorothy Gookin (quoted in *Good Wives* by Laurel Thatcher Ulrich) and from *The Diary of Matthew Patten of Bedford, N.H.*

"The Obstetrician's Lesson": The text in this poem is from *Woman; Her Diseases and Remedies*, 2nd ed., by Charles D. Meigs, who was known as a leader in the field of obstetrics in the nineteenth century. He was opposed to the use of obstetric anesthesia and refused to believe that puerperal fever could be spread by doctors' hands. Doctors are gentlemen, Meigs argued, and "a gentleman's hands are clean."

"The Doll in the Convent": I learned about the artwork made by nuns in the seventeenth through the nineteenth centuries in the catalog that accompanied the exhibition "Quilling: Devotional Creations from Cloistered Orders" at the Pinacoteca Giovanni e Marella Agnelli.

"Warp and Weft": The samplers mentioned in this poem (except for the Brontës') are part of the collection of the National Museum of American History. Sentences like "Nothing is known about the life of X" and "X has not yet been identified" appear on the museum's website. The phrase "with purpose or without" is quoted in "Needlework in the Lives and Novels of the Brontë Sisters," by Sally Hesketh. The quote from Charlotte Brontë is found in *Shirley*.

"Mary's Year": The text in this poem is from Mary L. Bowers's pocket diary from 1870. Bowers was twenty-one years old at the time and living in Granville, Massachusetts.

"Jane in the Interlude": The italicized phrases in this poem are from *A Child's Christmas in Wales* by Dylan Thomas.

"A Concept of Service": The text in this poem is from statements made by Diana Adams, George Balanchine, Suzanne Farrell, Melissa Hayden, Allegra Kent, Gelsey Kirkland, and Violette Verdy.

"Life-Sized Portrait": The text in this poem is from *Widow Basquiat* by Jennifer Clement.

"The Ballet Master": This poem is based on recollections of George Balanchine, mainly those found in *Balanchine's Ballerinas: Conversations with the Muses* by Robert Tracy with Sharon DeLano, and *I Remember Balanchine: Recollections of the Ballet Master* edited by Francis Mason.

"The Vocation of Saint Thérèse": The text in this poem is from *Story of a Soul: The Autobiography of Saint Thérèse of Lisieux*, 3rd ed., translated by John Clarke.

"Basic Reader": This poem reproduces a page from the *Elson-Gray Basic Readers: Pre-Primer* (1930), which was the first book to include the characters Dick and Jane.

"A Small Movement of Freedom inside of Fate": This poem sometimes quotes or paraphrases Paula Fox.

"Matisse's Great-Granddaughter, or Jane and the Long Way": The information in this poem is drawn from a variety of websites, articles, and books, including *Ways of Seeing* by John Berger; *Pleasure Painting: Matisse's Feminine Representations* by John Elderfield; *Matisse on Art* edited by Jack Flam; *Matisse: Father and Son* by John Russell; and *The Unknown Matisse: A Life of Henri Matisse: The Early Years, 1869–1908* by Hilary Spurling.

ACKNOWLEDGMENTS

THANK YOU TO THE editors of the following journals in which these poems, sometimes in earlier versions or with different titles, first appeared: *Alaska Quarterly Review*, "Matisse's Great-Granddaughter, or Jane and the Long Way"; *Barrow Street*, "The Ballet Master"; *The Common*, "Examples of the Interrogative in Jane's Kitchen"; *Copper Nickel*, "A Small Movement of Freedom inside of Fate"; *Denver Quarterly*, "Carte Blanche"; *Gettysburg Review*, "A Guide to Jane's Office"; *Mid-American Review*, "The Art Room" and "The Doll in the Convent"; *Pleiades*, "Diagnosis: Jane" and "Jane and the Escapes"; *The Sewanee Review*, "Einstein's Dinner," "Jane and the Bushel," "Seven Students," "Jane's Shame," "Jane in the Guest Room," "Basic Reader," "The Pedestal," "Jane in the Passenger Seat," "Questions on Jane's Birthday," excerpts from "Mary's Year" ("Wait," "Wealth," "Weather," "Wherewithal," "Woe," "World," "Worth"), "Jane and the Visitors," and "Jane's Souvenir"; *Tupelo Quarterly*, "The Vocation of Saint Thérèse." "The Pedestal" and "Jane in the Passenger Seat" also appeared on *Poetry Daily*.

I am grateful to the Ohio Arts Council for financial support during the writing of these poems. For selecting my manuscript for publication, and for her generous, incisive suggestions about it, deep thanks to Brenda Shaughnessy. Thank you to James McCoy, Karen Copp, Susan Hill Newton, Charlotte Wright, and everyone at the University of Iowa Press for their care in making this book. For important insights and encouragement, thank you to Sheila Black, Maria Hummel, Laura Micciche, Adam Ross, and Eric Smith. For various forms of support, thank you to my family.

Thank you to my daughters, Alice and Claire Bachelder, for inspiring and improving me. Daily, abiding thanks to Chris Bachelder, who in so many ways made this book possible.

IOWA POETRY PRIZE AND
EDWIN FORD PIPER POETRY AWARD WINNERS

1987
Elton Glaser, *Tropical Depressions*
Michael Pettit, *Cardinal Points*

1988
Bill Knott, *Outremer*
Mary Ruefle, *The Adamant*

1989
Conrad Hilberry, *Sorting the Smoke*
Terese Svoboda, *Laughing Africa*

1990
Philip Dacey, *Night Shift at the Crucifix Factory*
Lynda Hull, *Star Ledger*

1991
Greg Pape, *Sunflower Facing the Sun*
Walter Pavlich, *Running near the End of the World*

1992
Lola Haskins, *Hunger*
Katherine Soniat, *A Shared Life*

1993
Tom Andrews, *The Hemophiliac's Motorcycle*
Michael Heffernan, *Love's Answer*
John Wood, *In Primary Light*

1994
James McKean, *Tree of Heaven*
Bin Ramke, *Massacre of the Innocents*
Ed Roberson, *Voices Cast Out to Talk Us In*

1995
Ralph Burns, *Swamp Candles*
Maureen Seaton, *Furious Cooking*

1996
Pamela Alexander, *Inland*
Gary Gildner, *The Bunker in the Parsley Fields*
John Wood, *The Gates of the Elect Kingdom*

1997
Brendan Galvin, *Hotel Malabar*
Leslie Ullman, *Slow Work through Sand*

1998
Kathleen Peirce, *The Oval Hour*
Bin Ramke, *Wake*
Cole Swensen, *Try*

1999
Larissa Szporluk, *Isolato*
Liz Waldner, *A Point Is That Which Has No Part*

2000
Mary Leader, *The Penultimate Suitor*

2001
Joanna Goodman, *Trace of One*
Karen Volkman, *Spar*

2002
Lesle Lewis, *Small Boat*
Peter Jay Shippy, *Thieves' Latin*

2003
Michele Glazer, *Aggregate of Disturbances*
Dainis Hazners, *(some of) The Adventures of Carlyle, My Imaginary Friend*

2004
Megan Johnson, *The Waiting*
Susan Wheeler, *Ledger*

2005
Emily Rosko, *Raw Goods Inventory*
Joshua Marie Wilkinson, *Lug Your Careless Body out of the Careful Dusk*

2006
Elizabeth Hughey, *Sunday Houses the Sunday House*
Sarah Vap, *American Spikenard*

2008
Andrew Michael Roberts, *something has to happen next*
Zach Savich, *Full Catastrophe Living*

2009
Samuel Amadon, *Like a Sea*
Molly Brodak, *A Little Middle of the Night*

2010
Julie Hanson, *Unbeknownst*
L. S. Klatt, *Cloud of Ink*

2011
Joseph Campana, *Natural Selections*
Kerri Webster, *Grand & Arsenal*

2012
Stephanie Pippin, *The Messenger*

2013
Eric Linsker, *La Far*
Alexandria Peary, *Control Bird Alt Delete*

2014
JoEllen Kwiatek, *Study for Necessity*

2015
John Blair, *Playful Song Called Beautiful*
Lindsay Tigue, *System of Ghosts*

2016
Adam Giannelli, *Tremulous Hinge*
Timothy Daniel Welch, *Odd Bloom Seen from Space*

2017
Alicia Mountain, *High Ground Coward*
Lisa Wells, *The Fix*

2018
Cassie Donish, *The Year of the Femme*
Rob Schlegel, *In the Tree Where the Double Sex Sleeps*

2019
William Fargason, *Love Song to the Demon-Possessed Pigs of Gadara*
Jennifer Habel, *The Book of Jane*